Within" takes you on a personal journey of self-discovery and leaves you with feelings of hope but also gives you actionable steps to bring great things into your life! What an empowering delight." - Kimball Stadler, Provost, MountaintopUniversity.com

THE 12 POWERS WE HOLD WITHIN
The Ultimate Paradigm Shift

Orly Amor

Reviews for Orly Amor's
The Twelve Powers We Hold Within

"Definitely not your average self-help book, Orly Amor's "The Twelve Powers We Hold Within" is the ultimate step-by-step guide for creating positive, immediate change in every area of our lives. Each page is filled with fresh inspiration and life-altering guidance which empowers us to cast aside limiting thought patterns and retrain our brains to function in a way that helps us achieve new heights of growth and success across the board. I highly recommend this book!" - Ivan Misner, Ph.D., NY Times Bestselling Author and Founder of BNI®

"'The Twelve Powers We Hold Within,' is a must read for anyone who wants to go to the next level. In this book you will be taken through a process that will help you kick out your negative habits and bring in the positive habits. You will also receive the practical tools that it takes to stay on the right track. You, the reader, are in for a real treat." - Omar Periu, Omar Periu International

"We all want the best life possible. Happiness, health,

financial security and love, are achievable for each of us, but many of us are not experiencing them at the level we desire and deserve. In "The Twelve Powers We Hold Within", Orly gives us an easy to follow, step-by-step, process on how to make your brain work for you not against you. The 'Twelve Powers' are our formula for success. This is a book that you will use as a resource and go back to throughout your life. Put this on your 'must read' list and get one for a friend, they will thank you. Bravo Orly...thank you for your commitment to making us all better." - Frank J. De Raffele Jr., New York Times Best Selling Author, Co-Author of Business Networking and Sex: Not what you Think!, CEO – Entrepreneurial Excellence Worldwide, Inc.

"Orly's book provides insight into why some people fail while others succeed. If you're in need of a 'Mental Makeover', "The Twelve Powers We Hold Within" provides a perfect starting point." - Victor Antonio

"An inspiring and uplifting book which allows the reader to take an introspective look at our everyday road blocks and find ways to change our views. "The Twelve Powers We Hold

The Twelve Powers We Hold Within

Orly Amor 2nd Edition
Copyright © 2017 Orly Amor. All rights reserved.
Published by Global Mentoring Center Publishing
Editor-in-Chief: L.E. Saba

This publication is designed to provide accurate and
authoritative information in regard to the subject matter
covered. It is sold with the understanding that the publisher is
not engaged in rendering legal, accounting, or other
professional services. If legal advice or other expert assistance
is required, the services of a competent professional should be
sought.

Library of Congress Cataloging in Publication Data
Amor, Orly
The Twelve Powers We Hold Within

ISBN-13: 978-0-9996791-2-8

1. Self-Empowerment   2 Self-Improvement   3. Motivational
4. Mindset

Printed in the United States of America
First Printing: July 2012

TO ORDER MORE COPIES OF

The Twelve Powers We Hold Within
'The Ultimate Paradigm Shift'

VISIT YOUR FAVORITE BOOK STORE

OR VISIT
WWW.GLOBALMENTORINGCENTER.COM

QUANTITY DISCOUNTS AVAILABLE

OR

FOR BOOK TOUR AND APPEARANCES BY

ORLY AMOR VISIT

WWW.ORLYAMOR.COM

TO REACH ORLY DIRECTLY

CALL 917-515-6803

ACKNOWLEDGEMENTS

To my friend Chris Adams, who believed in me before I believed in myself.

***

To my friend and speaking mentor Victor Antonio, thank you for your guidance from day one and for the inspiration and encouragement you have provided all these years. I will be forever grateful to you and your family.

***

To my writing mentor Ivan Misner, Founder of BNI Business Network International for creating a mentoring program and inviting authors to help his mentees.

***

To Serafino Maiorano, of Maiorano and Associates, the best financial planner ever, for believing in me enough to trust me with your long time clients and for helping me see every week that my mission was worth my journey. I was proud to have you give me away at my wedding.

***

To Shani and Roy Gill, you guys are the nephew and niece that showed me the true meaning of love and affection through the eyes of a child. Since you were little your notes and drawings of affection have lifted my spirit and showed me how much difference I can make in the world.

***

To my husband Alex Diamantopoulos, for loving me just the way I am, for standing by me in good times and challenging ones, and for showing me that simple is better when it comes to seeing the world. You are the love of my life.

***

To Victoria Schneps of Schneps Publications, thank you for believing in me and launching the *Oh Orly* Column and helping the community while going through your own challenges. Your story needs to be told because you are an inspirational woman who needs to be honored with the Go-Giver Award.

***

To my friend Elyse Kaplan, you are an inspiration to what I do every day, you have shown me that smiling is the best gift we can give every person that crosses our path and that perseverance and the will to change can be the only factor between failure and success.

***

To my friend Kristina Khilberg, thank you for opening my

eyes to the speaking world and what you can achieve with dedication to a cause. Thank you for your friendship and support and for believing in me no matter what.

***

To my adopted little sister Stephanie Spruyt, you are the best little sister anyone can have. Thank you for showing me how to shop and for proving to me that family does not have to be blood. To you and your husband Tim Seitz, a big thanks for bringing me to New York.

***

Jessica Daniel and Asnat Daniel Gill, you have been my best friends since birth and no one can ask for a better family. You have listened and supported me through all my struggles and reminded me time and time again to not give up no matter what life throws at me. For that I will always be grateful to you and your parents. Each of you is the one friend people need to have in their life. I will love and cherish you always.

***

To my Mom and Dad for giving me life. I know you did your best in raising me. I am stronger for it.

***

To my dear friend, client and colleague Gary Karp. Thank you for being there for me in good times and in bad and showing me that perseverance does pay off. Thank you for your friendship and support when I wanted to give up on being myself and proving to me time and time again that it is because of who I am, not what I am that people show up for me and love me.

***

To my new best friend Rayma Garraway, thank you for being there for me when nobody else was able to.

***

To Robert Shields and Sandy Friedel, for showing me love is possible at any age.

***

To Bert and Alexa Oliva and Team for being there for me when no one else would step up and making my dreams a reality by providing guidance and support through all my projects. Your level of integrity, wisdom and professionalism is what we need in our industry of Public Speakers, Authors and Coaches.

***

Thank you to all my clients, partners and friends, without your support and encouragement this journey would not be worth it. I know we are in the process of changing lives, working towards our goal of 200,000,000 worldwide in the next ten to twenty years.

TABLE OF CONTENTS

Foreword

After a grueling four-day seminar in San Diego, California I turned to Orly and said, "I know you're going to do great things." My name is Chris and I am a successful entrepreneur. I met Orly as I sat next to her at a convention of about 2,000 attendees and a dozen amazing presenters and motivational speakers.

We immediately became good friends and spent time talking about our past experiences, relationships and business dealings. Being entrepreneurs has its ups and downs like anything else. Orly shared her passion for The Law of Attraction and how she can manifest anything into her immediate reality. As I listened to her and got to know her better, it was obvious she was meant to follow her passion, helping people all over the world.

The conference and our mutual businesses revolved around real estate and how to flip properties. I could see that Orly's heart was excited about learning, yet she and I knew neither of us was going to put all that information into practice.

On the first day of the conference the host announced they would be choosing three people from the audience to sing karaoke. All willing participants needed to do was sign-up and choose a song from a predetermined list.

The singers would be performing on the last day of the conference. Orly turned to me and said, "I would love to be on that stage. I have my own back-up music CDs with me." I replied almost immediately, "There will be many people on that list and they are only choosing three." She responded, "Yeah, you're probably right. Chances are slim."

On the last day of the conference the crowd happily acknowledged the courage of those who were called up to the stage, first one singer then a second one, both of which were very good.

As this was going on, Orly disappeared for a few minutes. When she got back she put her digital camera in front of her, I thought maybe she would like to have a couple of souvenir pictures since this conference, although very inspiring, was emotionally draining. She turned to me and said, "Just in case I go on that stage, can I show you how this camera works?" I replied, "Sure, did you put your name on the list?" I asked surprised by her request. She said "No, but just in case. I spoke with the MC and he said he would check."

I could not believe what I just heard; she went directly to the source? The next thing we hear is the MC over the microphone call out, "Where is Orly, that smiling young girl? Where are you Orly?" Orly jumped out of her seat and shouted, "Right here!"

The next thing I knew she was on stage singing and I was filming the whole thing. The crowd jumped to their feet and clapped their hands. Orly is on all the big projector screens everyone can see her. They are all dancing and clapping and the MC is smiling from ear to ear, proud to have chosen her. I did not know what came over me - I just started tearing up from joy, like a proud father.

When Orly came back to her seat and the excitement subsided, I turned to her and said, "How did you do it? How did you get that MC to let you on the stage without signing-up?" Her reply was, "Chris, I told you that I wanted to be on that stage from the moment they announced it. I also listened to you when you said there would be many people on that list. I did not let that stop me from visualizing myself on that stage. I just called on the universe to show me how, then I listened to the answer and I seized the opportunity. When the MC was by himself next to the DJ booth, I went to see him, knowing I only had about thirty seconds to capture his attention. I told him that I sing, I have my own back-up music CD, and if he lets me on that stage he won't be disappointed. I also told him he will be a hero and will be fulfilling one of my own dreams, to sing in front of a large crowd. That's it. Proving again, that the Law of Attraction works."

For those of you who don't know what the Law of Attraction is, there is a book called *The Secret* by

Rhonda Byrnes, and many other books that have been written about the subject where like attracts like and hence the likelihood of great things happening to happier and positive people as opposed to sadder and negative people.

"The Speech" by Chris Adams

"Thank you so much, that was an awesome speech," one woman said. "Thank you so much! I can't wait to go home and start applying what I learned today," another woman added. "You are wonderful, I loved your energy as soon as I saw you," a third attendee said excitedly. "Wow, your enthusiasm is contagious, thank you for sharing and inspiring all of us," yet another audience member stated while wiping away tears of joy.

The crowd gathered around Orly after she gave one of her workshops. Overwhelmed by her speech and her story, people felt compelled to let her know how much she changed their lives in such a short period of time. Many of them were wondering if she was going to write a book about her experiences. I too was thinking, "Why not, why shouldn't Orly write a book?"

That morning, Orly had woken up and looked around her home for some inspiration to start the day. One of her morning rituals is to go around the house and read the yellow Post-It notes she places here and here and on which she writes a few favorite affirmations with a black Sharpie so she could see them from anywhere in the house.

Then looking at the pool, at her Florida home she saw a frog struggling to climb out of the deep end of the pool. "That frog," she thought, "is me, he wants to get out of his predicament as much as I do" wondering how she would present her speech that evening in front of several hundred people. "What if they don't like me? What if they don't think what I say is valuable to changing their lives?"

Later that evening, after hearing all the applause and testimonials negating those exact fears,

Orly realized that she was on the right track to fulfilling her mission.

As an attendee and a friend of Orly's, I thought again, "She needs to write a book about all of this."

After leaving the event on that September night, Orly and I got into the car and after a few moments of silence she asked, "So what did you think?" I said, "Well, you heard them. They loved you." Not satisfied with my answer, as I knew she wouldn't be, she replied, "Yes I heard them, but I want to know your opinion."

Orly likes to get to the point and gets annoyed if you don't. Knowing that and knowing not to give my opinion unless asked, I was happy that she did. In my mind I thought it was a perfect time to suggest writing the book "I think you should write a book. I think you should tell your story. I think you should practice what you preach and pay it forward." I said it with conviction. Orly's reply was pretty immediate. "Me? Write a book? I don't know the first thing about writing a book. Where do I start? How do I know people will want to read my book? And what makes me so different than any other book or story out there?"

Having known Orly for a few years I asked her, "How did all this start for you? How did you come up with a way to overcome all those challenges in your life?"

So there we were, both silently contemplating these questions when Orly responded, "Alright I'll do it, I will write a book that not only tells my story, but a book that when individuals read it, they will think I am right there by their side – they need to feel that I truly care about them and they need to have immediate results after reading the book. Fair enough?" I replied, "Fair enough. Let me know when it comes out."

-- Chris Adams, July 2012

A LETTER TO MY NEW FRIEND

Dear Friend,

I discovered the art of public speaking and found myself a mentor in 2002. I paid thousands of dollars to be mentored.

To make sure I respected the audience, offering them the value they wanted, I gave 150% with every speech and never assumed anything. This was hard and I realized how much I did not know about public speaking, something that I am so passionate about. I began to speak about property management in seminars. I also attended Toastmasters meetings where I spoke about my life and the lessons I learned.

I soon realized that my talks about my life lessons had to be communicated strongly. I needed someone to help me go from a 'Simple Citizen of the Republic' to a fierce "Jedi knight' (* terms referencing the Star Wars series). So began my search for a person who could fit the bill. In June 2008, I found a mentor that belonged to a few "secret societies," where only men are allowed and where everything discussed stays within the society. "Can you keep a secret and never tell a soul until the day you die, Orly?"

"Yes, of course. What would that secret be?" I asked.

"Well," my mentor said. "You have to promise first that you not tell the source of what I am going to share with you."

I immediately responded, "I promise with all my heart that whatever it is you want me to keep secret, I will." Mind you, I was introduced to this man by very reputable businessmen so my word had to stand firm.

My journey as a learner, as an apprentice, began. I was not to ever tell a soul where I received my information, and I promised to pay it forward to whoever wanted to listen to these words. I trained, and read, and did homework, and was questioned at every occasion on what I had learned. How many people's lives I touched in a day, and again, what I had learned.

A year or so later, a traumatic business experience had me fall into a depressive state. I truly did not know which way was up, or what I would do next. I will share my story with you later on in the book.

The experience led me to question, "Why Me? Why Now? Where did this come from? Why did I not see this coming? How am I going to live? How am I going to get through this when all the odds are against me?" I think you clearly get the point.

I was introduced to a few programs and studied each one of them from beginning to end. Books, I read cover to cover. CDs and DVDs, I listened to some ten times, some 100 times, and one of them, The Secret, over a thousand times and that is no exaggeration. In fact, I still listen to many of them today.

Now I ask you, how many times have you bought a book and put it on the shelf after the first or

second chapter? How many times have you bought a
set of CDs only to listen to them once and then say,
"I'll come back to this later?" I will fully admit that
this was me 20 years ago.

I became a seminar junkie and a
procrastinator at the same time. Do you know anyone
like that? You, maybe? I bought something at every
seminar and some of the things I purchased never
even came out of their packaging. Until I met my
mentor who encouraged me to stop procrastinating
and go back to everything I already had at my
fingertips. If only I had known! Think of all the
money I could have saved (not to mention all of those
hours sitting on uncomfortable folding chairs in hotel
conference rooms).

After going through the readings, listening and
observing those I looked up to in envy and with
pride, and because now I know that everything I have
been through and learned, has led me to this
innovative idea to pay it forward. It became my
obsession. I asked my mentor to show me how I

could reduce the amount of time to learn all this. Nobody has that much time on their hands these days to read all the books and to listen to all the CDs.

I knew I was overwhelmed as I became a full time student of the subject, but something was missing. I had very little patience and I wanted to make it happen right away. Show me!

I had a long conversation with my mentor where he tried to convince me that it was impossible to do that, and if somehow I found a way, it still wouldn't work.

"I am going to create the program," I told him.

"Call me when it's complete." He didn't seem convinced.

Six months later I called and he invited me over to show him my work. Sixteen hours later, exhausted and defeated, my mentor said, "If I can't talk you out of it, this means your passion and your beliefs are unbreakable. After all this time of me questioning you on every minute detail of your plan, and you answering with the same drive, your plan is as solid as can be, and you have my blessing."

Wow, sixteen hours of torturous questions with the most negative notions of, "What ifs" and "What will you do, if?" I realized I had something special and I wanted to share it with the world.

The combination of *The Secret*, *The Red Pill*, *What the [Bleep] Do We Know?*, *The Ma*trix, *What Dreams May Come*, *Star Wars*, *Think and Grow Rich*, *Rich Dad, Poor Dad*, *The Power of Positive Thinking*, *Your Wish is Your Command*, *The Four* and *The Five Agreements* – all books, movies, DVDs, and CDs related to these subjects, are missing one element which I will reveal to you in this book.

Introduction

The Twelve Powers We Hold Within is a concept that is designed for individuals who are struggling with a traumatic experience that is disabling them from going forward in life. Its sole purpose is to identify the individual qualities and gifts that are inherent to each and every one of us and to point out the unique abilities that we all possess to help us be, do, or have anything we want in life.

There are many books and great works out there to help with such life challenges. Never before was it put in laymen's words, given in simple to follow, step-by-step, day-by-day, exercises to help you achieve your goals and dreams. Secret societies and other organizations guide their own to success, and this book is for those who want to be of the movement that helps anyone willing to take a step into being the best they can be and paying it forward.

In this book you will discover what it is that makes you unique right from the moment you were born up to wherever you may be in life. Whether you are happy or not with your current situation is irrelevant. Reading and putting into practice the exercises from this book will immediately change your circumstances. You will learn how to give your undivided attention to your goals and achieve them one at a time.

Never make excuses again.

In the first chapter you will identify the excuses you have been giving yourself, making them your reality, not to mention the excuses you give other people when you become defensive about your circumstances and are looking to validate your thinking.

What you are not aware of is that you have

created neuro-pathways that have now grown into deep roots in your mind and get stronger every time you talk about your situation. You will learn how to break the habit that has been created in your mind and follow simple exercises to interrupt the negative neuro-pathways in order to reach your goals. With practice these neuro-pathways can be changed.

You will also learn about the Negative and Positive sides of yourself and the difference each makes in your thought process.

A Little Bit About Me

All the roads we travel eventually bring us to our ultimate destination, our now.

Sometimes you have to go through difficult detours. Then again, at other times, the road is straight and smooth. Keep in mind that each and every one of these turns, twists and detours is an opportunity to learn a little something about yourself. It's an opportunity to tweak things and redirect life.

Look at it as your training ground to your ultimate destination – your best life ever!

Allow me to briefly share with you my own journey to now.

It all started when I was a little girl. My parents were hard working, middle class people who did what everyone else did at the time - get married and have kids in order not to live with their parents anymore.

They drilled a few thoughts into me early on. I was told that life is hard; that I can't get what I want because life is not always easy, and that some things are just impossible because we are not rich. Does this sound familiar? I'll bet it does.

When I wanted to go outside and play with the other kids, I often heard "NO!" I had to beg and promise to do chores in order to get what I wanted, to go out and play.

If the chores I did were not to my mother's ideal of perfection she would beat me. I have a vivid memory of a beautiful, sunny day when I was six years old. I thought I would wash the dishes to surprise my mom. I broke a glass. Instead of being happy I did the dishes for her, my mom became furious I broke the glass. She grabbed a shoe and gave me a memorable beating. Punishment for mistakes like these was either getting hit repeatedly with a wooden hanger or with my Dad's big metal belt buckle – pick one, let me assure you they were equally painful.

School was another nightmare. I had trouble keeping clean out of fear of asking to go to the bathroom and being punished. I wet the bed until I was 14 because of that fear. At least I did not get a beating for that.

To make matters worse, friends were scarce and did not want to hang out with me.

I thought the only way I could get friends was to buy their friendship, so I gave away my toys. I even gave away my mom's treasured pen collection. Every day I would take a few pens to school and give them to my friends. The pens were not of any value. She kept what seemed to me to be a few hundreds of them in a square silver box. They ranged from the common Bic or Paper Mate types to more expensive ones.

The day my mother noticed that precious pen box was almost empty, she gave me the beating of my life. She hit me with everything she could grab -

shoes, the big belt buckle *and* the wooden hanger, switching from one to the other, until her hands tired and she finally stopped. My posterior sported all the colors of the rainbow, there were even a few that had not yet been invented.

The next day in school I was in so much pain I could not sit. The teacher did not believe my story and made me stand in the corner all day, facing the wall.

The only person in school that seemed empathetic to all of the problems I was going through was our school janitor. One day he asked if I wanted some peanuts. As I reached for them, he grabbed me and put his hands where he shouldn't have and rubbed his private parts on me. It was very scary. But I was eventually able to free myself. This kept happening all through second grade. He threatened me and said that no one would believe me if I told on him.

Before I reached the age of 14, four different men molested me several times each. One of these men was a family member. When I got the courage to tell my mom that my grandfather had been abusing me for four years. She told me to never tell anyone, especially not my father. I felt betrayed and ashamed. She also said that if I had shared that with her sooner she would not have let my grandfather back in our house.

At the age of 16, I ran away from home, sort of. My family visited Wildwood, New Jersey every summer and I used to see some of my friends from school working on the boardwalk. That inspired me to plan my exit. My parents would give my brother and I money to go to the arcades and the amusement park every day, but instead of taking advantage of this and enjoying myself, I looked for a job and a place to stay.

Two days before my family was to return home, I announced that I would not be going back with them. I would be staying in Wildwood for the remainder of the summer. After showing them where I would work and live, their only words were,

"If you don't like it here, you can take the bus back home." In my mind I was thinking, "Yeah right, like that's going to happen!"

I worked hard, saved money, and lived in a rooming house. The neighbors on the first floor were really nice guys from Pennsylvania and I became very fond of one of them – the wrong one unfortunately. Wrong, because when he wanted to get intimate I told him that I had never shared myself with anyone before, he did not believe me and raped me. When he was done, he said he would kill me if I ever told anyone or called the police.

In my late teens I was gang raped twice, nine months apart. The first time was by people I knew, the second time by complete strangers.

I was married to a mentally and physically abusive husband. By the age of 22 I decided the relationship had to end and I proceeded to get a divorce.

The trauma of these experiences led me to gain a tremendous amount of weight - reaching 428 pounds by the age of 22.

Morbidly obese, dating online, and attracting the wrong types of men, all because my self-worth and self-esteem were so very low, I knew I had to do something. I started going to seminars that were amazingly motivating and inspiring.

That's when I chose to heal myself. I watched every video I could get my hands on: Tony Robbins, Omar Periu, and Les Brown. I went to all their seminars. I've spent over $250,000 on books, CD's, and conferences. I threw everything I had into my work and became a workaholic. I focused on the future, but didn't share about my past.

I did everything I could just to have what these speakers had: money, cars, and vacation homes.

All that learning was great for about two weeks. I listened and read, read and listened. I applied what I could understand to be right for me. I got to learn quite a few things, but not necessarily the ones that would make long lasting changes, not the ones that would keep me on track, and certainly not the ones that would provide instant results to motivate me to continue.

I was frustrated and desperately looking for a better solution. *There must be something missing in all of these programs.*

I found out I was not the only one struggling with this thought, many people had experienced similar outcomes.

It is proven that 97% of people who buy motivational programs don't even make it past the first chapter or the first CD. Two percent read the book cover to cover or listen to the complete CD set and only 1% actually put into practice what they learned. This 1% are the ones that got some result, giving them a sense of satisfaction. That's the reason so many self-help books are being written and many more CDs/DVDs produced and sold every day.

You are probably saying, "Okay Orly, I hear you. So what makes your program any different than all the rest?"

I'm so glad you asked. You see, very few of the

programs out there teach you about your mind. None of the programs out there give you an understanding of how you are programmed; and none mention what it is that makes you tick.

Yes, it *does* take some understanding of how your mind works before you can learn and apply new ways of thinking, new ways of being, and to help change the course of your journey from a difficult one to a smoother, more enjoyable one.

Think of your brain as a computer. Let me assure you that you have been programmed since childhood. I suspect you know this, but did you know that you are still being programmed? Software is constantly being added to an already overloaded hard drive. Worse still is that a lot of the information stored in your mind is not serving you to live your best life.

Do I have your attention?

You see, I overcame that programming. I was able to lose 172 pounds, finish my Masters in Business Administration, and became a successful entrepreneur traveling to 26 countries and 18 States.

My own struggles and the success I experienced by applying what I learned led me to write this book and share my journey with you to help you change your own life's journey into your best life ever.

My accolades are not as important as my ability to help you change course in one go.

Thanks to my many speaking engagements, books, and one-on-one mentoring, I can guarantee immediate results.

That is my promise to you, and I am willing to back it up. Change *will* happen after you read the first two chapters.

Are you with me? Let's get started!

You may or may not know that I was in property management for over 25 years and was an entrepreneur, author, speaker and consultant in this field. But what most of you do not know is my personal journey of the past 20 years and the shocking truths life revealed to me.

Having been through so many ups and downs, I've gone from financial security to broke and back again, like a yo-yo. Many of my close friends called me a survivor. So whenever I would say to them, "Guess what happened?" Their response would be, "Yeah, yeah but by this time next year we will be laughing about this," and they were right.

I attended many seminars and motivational workshops, read the books (some of which you will see listed in the Recommended Reading List) and reread them all a few times. I learned so much and soon realized that this knowledge cannot only be for me, it must be shared. And so the desire to give back to the world was birthed within me.

When I shared my vision with my friends about becoming the next Mother Theresa they laughed and said, "You're crazy, but if anyone can do it, it is you."

Part One - The Brain

"Minds are like parachutes; they work best when open."
- Lord Thomas Dewar

Let's start by investigating some rumors about how the brain works:

True or false: The brain's hippocampus, the part of the brain believed to be the center of emotion and memory, contains an "Oprah neuron" that lights up when we see pictures of Ms. Winfrey or when we hear her name. If you guessed "false," check out British neuroscientist Rodrigo Quian Quiroga's study, which not only found specialized Oprah neurons, but also found brain cells devoted to Jennifer Aniston, Halle Berry, basketball great Michael Jordan, and even the character Luke Skywalker. There were also nerve cells that preferred watching *The Simpsons* to listening to Madonna's music.

While the study was small, involving seven epileptic patients with electrodes implanted in their brains to find cells that were triggering their seizures, the research offers an intriguing look at the mysteries hidden inside our brains, which contain more neurons than the galaxies in the known universe: about 100 billion on average, plus thousands of miles of nerves, packed into a space about the size of a coconut.

Each brain is unique, no two are alike—not even those of identical twins.

According to NeuroHealth & Associates - Center for Neurofeedback, there are a few myths about the brain. Let's take a look at five common brain myths and see if we can debunk them.

Myth # 1: We Only Use 10% of Our Brain.

Brain imaging studies using PET scans and MRIs show that any mentally complex activity uses many areas of the brain. Over the course of a day just about all of the brain gets a workout.

The fact that the entire brain is crucial to daily life is proven by the devastating impact of damage to even a small area. We do, however, have some mental capacity in reserve.

Studies of autopsies found that senior citizens who stay mentally active, through activities like reading the newspaper, solving word puzzles, going to the theater, or playing chess, are less likely to develop Alzheimer's disease—even if they have the characteristic physical brain changes typical of dementia, suggesting that mental function has a "use it or lose it" component.

This allows people who keep their brain stimulated to develop more brain reserves, allowing them to continue functioning normally, even as their brain is suffering damage caused by Alzheimer's.

Myth #2: People are Right-brained or Left-brained.

You've probably heard that left-brained people are logical and good at solving problems, while right-brained people are imaginative and artistic. This myth began in the 1800's, when doctors discovered that injury to one side of the brain frequently caused a loss of specific abilities to the other side of the body. Brain scan experiments, however, show that the two halves of the brain are intricately linked, much more than was originally thought, so problem-solving or creative tasks fire up activity in regions in both hemispheres of the brain, not just half. It is true that the right side of the brain controls the left side of the body and vice versa, so a right-brain injury can cause disability on the left side of the body.

Myth #3: Your Brain is Gray.

You've probably seen preserved brains on TV or in a science classroom that look gray or yellowish white. Although the living brain is sometimes described as "gray matter," it may be gray but it also contains "white matter" (nerve cells that link the gray matter), red areas (due to many blood vessels that feed the brain), and a black area colored by neuromelanin, a form of the melanin pigment found in skin and hair. Preserved brains turn solid gray because they're soaked in chemicals like formaldehyde.

Myth #4: "Flashbulb Memories" are Like Photocopies of Events.

We all have vivid memories of dramatic events, such as being in a car accident or what we were doing when the Twin Towers fell. _Smithsonian Magazine_ reports that while recollections may feel extremely precise, studies show that they can be surprisingly inaccurate because our mind can play tricks on us. For example, a study cited in this report found that 73 percent of college students "remember" watching Live TV coverage of the first plane hitting the North Tower on 9/11. In reality, the

South Tower was hit first and neither event was televised live.

Myth #5: Our Brains are Less Sharp After 40.

Actually, mental agility starts to slip when we're in our late 20s, according to a study published in the journal *Neurobiology of Aging*. When researchers tested 2,000 healthy adults, they found that brain speed and reasoning skills (as measured by tests that involved solving puzzles, recalling words and story details, and spotting patterns) peak at age 22, then start a slow decline at age 27.

Some mental skills, however, do improve with age. Older people have larger vocabularies, are better judges of character, and score higher on social skills tests, such as how to resolve a dispute. They also outperform the young on remembering images and phrases that evoke positive emotions, which may explain why surveys show that, on average, older people are happier.

Cool stuff, right?

If at any moment while reading the above you said or thought, "Wow" or "Hmmmm, how interesting," that is already a paradigm shift happening in your brain. I will refer to paradigm shifts often in this book so you can recognize what they are and what it feels like when it happens. All you've got to do is trust in the process. Now, isn't that easy?

A note of caution is necessary at this point before we continue on. This book is not for everybody. Before going further you need to answer two questions. One, are you open minded enough to learn? And two, are you willing to welcome change?

You might be very comfortable where you currently are. If that's the case, you may resist the new ideas I will be presenting to you throughout this book. You need to be uncomfortable and have the desire to change more than anything else in order to experience change.

Both of your answers to these questions MUST be yes.

At this point, I'd like you to read the following exercise and complete it before continuing on. This exercise is crucial to the whole premise of the book.

Close your eyes and imagine two cartoon images.

One looks like a huge beach ball with the scariest face you can imagine, a face that if it actually appeared in front of you right now would frighten you.

The second cartoon image is quite smaller maybe the size of a Ping Pong ball and it has a very sad face. It looks so sad, like a child who lost his puppy and you feel very sorry for this child.

Now, close your eyes. Imagine those two cartoons. When you have a vivid picture of them in your mind I want you to open your eyes and draw them on a piece of paper as best you can. There is a very good reason to do this, I promise. I'll explain a bit later.

Here is an example of what mine look like:

The
Negative Ball

The Positive Ball

Before I clarify exactly what the Negative and Positive Balls represent, I want to give you some fundamental rules of how your brain actually works. This may be a bit of a refresher for some and new information for others.

We have over seventy thousand thoughts each and every day.

The thoughts we can control are in our frontal cortex, in the forefront of the brain. These are our conscious thoughts and reside in the conscious mind, the part of our brain that is responsible for logic and reasoning. Most of our thoughts though are subconscious. This is where our emotions are seated.

But wait there's more.

Here are some rules to guide you as we move forward. I will keep reminding you of them as we progress through the book.

Do I still have your attention? Good!

The Way Our Brain Works

1. Knowledge is Power

There are four ways the brain processes new information:

a. You don't know what you don't know. (Unconscious Incompetence). *When you were a baby you had no idea that one day you would need to know how to lace up shoes.*

b. You know what you don't know. (Conscious Incompetence) *I don't know how to drive an 18-wheeler so if you see me at the wheel of one stay clear of the road!*

c. You know what you know. (Conscious Competence). *You know how to read otherwise you wouldn't be reading this book right now.*

d. You do things automatically. (Unconscious

Competence). *If I ask you to tie your shoelaces today would you need to think about it? No.*

One example to illustrate how you can reach Unconscious Competence is with driving. When you learned how to drive, you started with Conscious Incompetence ("I don't know how to drive.") After lessons, you began to have Conscious Competence ("By focusing really hard, I can drive the car by paying close attention to every detail of all that is around me.") Once you start to feel confident in your driving abilities, you will reach a state of Unconscious Competence. Ever think, "How did I get here?" after a long drive even though you arrived at your destination safely?

2. The Mind does not know the difference between a truth and a lie

Whatever it is you're thinking your mind perceives it to be a certainty.

Perception is a reality that you create for yourself. A good example is the emotion called

F.E.A.R.

FEAR = Fictional Elements Appearing Real.

The emotion of fear is created by the unknown and brings us back to, "You don't know what you don't know." (Unconscious Incompetence)

Don't let that confuse you. It will all come together very soon.

3. Good or bad, right or wrong, do not exist in the universe

The only time this statement can be true is when you say, "This is good for me" or "This is wrong for me." Otherwise they do not exist.

To prove this theory, I can say that something is good for me while you could say that the very same thing is bad for you, and vice versa. So, which one of us is right, which is wrong? Neither, it simply applies to the event or circumstances and how you or I perceive it to be true.

4. Control your thoughts or at least the

ones you know of

How can I illustrate a thought?

A thought is like a seed planted in your brain. What happens to a seed when you give it air, water and sunlight? It grows roots and it becomes a very nice plant with strong roots to keep it grounded. What happens to a seed when you shield it from the sun and don't give it any water? It dies.

So every time you have a thought, neurons anchor it in your brain and eventually root it into your subconscious mind. Our thoughts create our feelings, and our feelings are anchored into our subconscious mind. Remember the exercise about the two cartoon balls? Do you know what we did? We created a thought that became an image that in turn created a feeling or an emotion.

When I asked you to draw those images on a piece of paper, the simple act of drawing, or writing anything for that matter, creates an anchor in your mind. Think about this, what controls your hand? Your brain does. So from time to time I will ask you to write things down for this very reason, to create anchors.

Throughout the book, I will be using these simple rules and metaphors about how the brain works to help illustrate the points I'm communicating.

If you followed me up to now, you are doing amazingly well and are on the right track. Shall we continue on our journey?

Did you learn something so far? Did I pique your interest?

Great! Another paradigm shift in your brain has occurred without you even realizing it. I will prove this to you later.

How cool is that?

Part Two - The Positive and Negative Balls

"Whether you think you can, or whether you think you can't, you are always right."
Henry Ford, father of the American automotive assembly line.

Remember your two cartoons? Do you still have that vivid picture in your mind? Do you still have your drawings? Good!

The Negative Ball

The Negative Ball contains all events, circumstances, things said and things heard, all your fears, all of your emotions: anxiety, worry, boredom, frustration, disappointment, sadness, guilt, and shame. It is made up of your imagination, memories of things that happened to you, actions you did to others or that were done to you, good or bad, right or wrong, lies or truths, dreams, and nightmares.

The Negative Ball has programs that were put there both long ago and recently. For example:

- Times are hard.
- The economy is bad.
- Only rich people get rich.
- You're better off with the devil you know then the one you don't.
- A bird in the hand is worth two in the bush.
- Money doesn't grow on trees.
- You have to work hard to get anywhere in life.
- You have to start at the bottom and work your way up.
- You can't put the horse before the carriage.
- Do you think I'm made out of money?
- It takes money to make money.

The 12 Powers We Hold Within

- And so many more....

Your Negative Ball feeds on all these things. He has a party every time you feel these emotions and worst of all, he will do everything in his power to keep you in that dark place. Everything in the Negative Ball is there to stay forever. None of the information put in there by you or anyone else can be deleted, erased, removed or destroyed. Now that is very scary and it's why the Negative Ball has such a frighteningly devilish look. If you're not scared now you will be once you learn more. Just remember this as being a true fact: Your Negative Ball is your worst enemy.

You are probably thinking to yourself, "Okay Orly, I hear you and I am getting pretty concerned about it. You say I can't undo this, what can I do to put a stop to my Negative Ball's partying?"

Answer: Nothing.

Now you are probably bordering on horrified, but all isn't lost. There's no need to panic. I assure you there is hope.

The only thing to do is keep the Negative Ball from growing. However old or young you may be at the moment, that is also your Negative Ball's age and he will keep on growing.

Your job is to stop it from expanding. Want to know how?

Before I tell you how to stop your Negative Ball from mushrooming, let me tell you about your Positive Ball. He needs more attention.

You forgot about him did you not?

The Positive Ball

The Positive Ball is very small and the only way I know how to explain what is in this little sphere is by having you go there in your mind.

Have you ever woken up in the morning and felt really good? You slept well, had a refreshing shower, and ate a delicious breakfast. You opened up the curtains, looked outside and saw it was a glorious day. Your heart filled with joy and bliss and you thought to yourself how wonderful it is to be alive and how amazing nature is. It is a wonderful, peaceful feeling and you just fall in love with yourself, your life, and the world. It is a marvelous feeling, is it not? Can you think of a moment like that?

This is the Positive Ball. He is all the wonderful feelings you have or have ever had. He is your self-confidence, your self-love, and your self-esteem. The Positive Ball fills you with courage and confidence to tackle any challenges that may come your way. He is your friend and wants the best for you.

Negative Ball vs. Positive Ball

But then the day starts to unravel. Around 10:00am, something happens and you start feeling angry and miserable. You feel sluggish and wish you didn't get out of bed that morning. The worst part is that you don't really know why you feel this way. That, my friend, is your Negative Ball. You see, the Negative and Positive Balls are always warring for control of your mind.

The Negative Ball feels your happiness and confidence and goes on the attack. He knows he will starve if you do not feed him so he says, "You can't feel good all day. Here are some negative anchors and thoughts that I handpicked just for the occasion. Enjoy the anxiety! Thank you for feeding me."

Your wonderful moments of happiness and joy and bliss? Those moments are stored in your Positive Ball. Unfortunately, most of us tend to focus on what might go wrong. We focus on the anxiety and fear. When we do this we feed the Negative Ball and he grows stronger. Our loyal friend, the Positive Ball feels left out. That's why he has a sorrowful face. It's your Positive Ball's mission to make you feel incredible, but by feeding the Negative Ball you rob the Positive Ball of his purpose.

The good news is, you can feel good every day. All day.

For those who are still skeptical, keep reading. I am about to blow your mind.

Every thought we have creates an anchor and

according to the five myths we talked about, we have billions of thoughts. If this is true, then we have many, many anchors. We create those anchors by the way we speak and the way we think every day.

Negative thoughts and words are what feeds and grows our Negative Ball and he is not going to stop growing any time soon unless … we will learn about this in another chapter.

Your Positive Ball is also craving thoughts. Good thoughts and great feelings so he can get nourished and grow increasingly stronger. He needs that strength to kick the Negative Ball out when it infiltrates your mind and kills your happy moments.

Imagine the Negative Ball as the kid sneaking behind your back to steal a cookie from the cookie jar. What happens when you catch the child? He gets startled and stops in his tracks.

By recognizing the kinds of thoughts/anchors you are creating every day you can stop the ones that don't serve you. What happens when you do this? You stop the Negative Ball from growing. It will stay the same size as long as you don't feed it.

You have been controlled like a puppet all your life by the thoughts and feelings anchored in your brain. This is the scary thought I was talking about earlier. You need to be scared knowing that you are not in control. Your Negative Ball is.

And that is only part of what is missing in the self-help books, CDs and DVDs out there. No one explains the what, who, why and how of reaching that beautiful life you want and deserve.

What is in our brain? Who put it there?

Why are we not operating at our maximum potential? How do we fix this?

You will find the answers to these questions in this book and you will be a changed person when you reach the last page. You will never be the same again and that is a promise.

As a matter of fact, if you learned anything so far, if you remembered anything from the previous pages, or if you have any interest or feelings of excitement and anticipation of learning more - you are already changed.

"All that is great Orly, but how do I do this? How do I stop the Negative ball from growing? And how do I feed the Positive Ball? Oh, and by the way, what about the Twelve Powers? When do we get to that?"

You must have patience my friend, patience. I need to take you step by step. My mission is to help you anchor concepts you can put into practice every day of your life. That is what will shape your future forever.

You're going to love this!

Self-Fulfilling Prophecy

The Self-Fulfilling Prophecy (SFP) is an important concept to understand in order to be able to forecast long-term consequences of current behavior. A "prophecy" is a prediction of upcoming events. "Self-fulfilling," means something occurs simply because the expectation exists.

In other words, the mere anticipation of an event greatly increases its likelihood of actually occurring. If you believe someone is a jerk, that mere expectation greatly increases the probability that he will "be" a jerk, at least, in your eyes.

So what does this concept mean to us?

Well, there are a few major points to consider:

- If you don't believe you are going to

close a sale, guess what?

• If you think your wife doesn't love you, guess what?

• If you really believe in yourself, do you think this belief, in and of itself, influences the way people respond to you?

Of course.

Your expectations greatly influence what happens in your life! That's why it pays to be an optimist rather than a pessimist. One way of thinking is not more right than the other. It simply means that better things are more likely to happen to an optimist.

This is one of the most important concepts to understand. It is the element that produces the greatest results in the shortest period of time. When you start to believe in yourself and what you can do, your productivity greatly increases and you start to become much more successful than you have ever been before in your life.

This is not "wishful" thinking. You can't just

hope for things to be better. You have to "believe" things are already better. That is the power of having a tool like this book, to give you insight. And the wonderful part is that results can last a lifetime.

Some examples Self-Fulfilling Prophecies are:

- "I never get a break."
- "I will never succeed."
- "This is too difficult."

Your negative thoughts and self-talk about yourself feed the Negative Ball. I am sure you realize this by now and you are on your way to speaking and thinking more positively about yourself.

The paradigm shifts in your brain are already happening and they will become bigger and bigger, each one becoming an "a-ha" moment.

So I have a question, what have you learned so far?

Did you have any "a-ha" moments?

The 12 Powers We Hold Within

"Every human has four endowments - self-awareness, conscience, independent will, and creative imagination. These give us the ultimate human freedom ... The power to choose, to respond, to change."

- Stephen Covey

Have you ever been in a situation where you were saddened, disappointed, or discouraged? How many of these situations, events, and circumstances still occupy you mind right now? The truth is that some of these situations, events, or circumstances are not around anymore. You might be facing different challenges; but the old ones are simply gone. As humans we are resilient creatures. It is human to fall down once in a while but we always get back up again. To be human is to be resilient. Inspired action steps are involved in your will to continue living. Yes, life is beautiful and it can be fun! Remember, you have the Powers within you to live up to your full potential. What you will discover in The Twelve Powers is that not only are you not alone, but that you are your own promise to a wonderful life.

The 12 Powers We Hold Within

1. The Power to Get Back Up
2. The Power of Attitude
3. The Power of Self-Talk
4. The Power of Honesty
5. The Power of Taking Action
6. The Power of Knowledge
7. The Power of Why
8. The Power of Determination
9. The Power of Forgiveness
10. The Power of Choice
11. The Power of Focus

12. The Power of Happiness

1. The Power to Get Back Up

"My attitude has always been, if you fall flat on your face, at least you're moving forward. All you need to do is get back up and try again."
- Richard Branson

I glanced at my watch and then up at the board. I found my flight and saw the angry letters were still there: DELAYED.

It was 8:30pm and I was stuck at JFK on a layover. My connecting flight back to Florida should have lifted off three hours ago. I glanced around and saw the other passengers milling about talking on their cell phones. *Let me text "Jane" and check in and make sure everything is fine.*

I tapped out a message on my iPhone, hit "send" and waited for the three dots in the balloon to appear. Ten minutes went by. Twenty minutes, no response came. After forty-five minutes I began to get worried.

What could have happened?

Is Jane okay? Did she get in an accident? Was she attacked? Was she sick?

Before I left on my latest business trip, I left Jane with the keys to the office, my car, and my home. As she was the bookkeeper for my firm, I also left her with a bunch of blank checks to pay the staff and handle any expenses that came up while I was out of town.

My phone rang. *Finally*, I thought and glanced to see who was calling me. It was not Jane but my ex-boyfriend.

"Hey hun, did you close the office?" He asked.

"What?"

"I drove by the office and it was completely dark."

My mind raced. *What was he talking about?* He probably drove by at night and no one was there. "When did you drive by?"

"I drove by a couple of times to check on it while you were away. There's been no action. It's dark."

"You must be mistaken. I'll handle it when I get back."

It was already past midnight when the cab came to a stop behind my BMW and I stepped out onto the driveway. The house was dark. The manicured lawn sweeping beyond the grey marble of the house looked like a dark green sea. Jane had finally texted me just before I boarded my connecting flight from JFK and told me my house and car keys were locked in the car's trunk. When I arrived at Ft. Lauderdale airport I was mad. I just wanted to go home and sleep but now I had to deal with this shit. I called AAA and sat down on my luggage to wait.

They arrived 45 minutes later. A large hispanic

man stepped out. "Looks like you got a problem," he smiled. "You locked your keys in the trunk, huh?"

"Something like that. Could you just open the trunk, please?"

He mumbled something. After grabbing a slim jim from his truck he walked to the driver side door. A few seconds later I heard the pop of the lock and my car door was open. "There you go, lady. That'll be fifty bucks."

"I thought it was included in the AAA service?"

"Oh yeah. You're with AAA. I forgot, sorry."

Everyone's a crook, I thought. I reached into my car and popped the trunk release.

I retrieved the keys from the trunk and headed for my front door. Looking at my house it seemed no worse for wear. I walked up the marble steps to my front door. I was so tired. *I wonder what I'll find inside.*

The first thing that hit me was the smell of dog poop. Jane was supposed to stop by the house to walk my dog while I was away. She never did and the house was covered in shit. It was all over the furniture and the floors. It was in the living room, the kitchen, my bedroom. Worse, my dog was covered in it as well. It was matted to his fur. I wanted to scream.

I really don't need this. All I wanted to do was take a hot shower and fall asleep. Instead, I found myself down on my hands and knees scrubbing shit off the floors. Afterwards, I gave the dog a bath and groomed him.

It was after two in the morning when I collapsed and fell into a fitful sleep.

Monday morning I arrived at the office prepared to have some choice words with Jane.

I unlocked my office door and walked inside. It was empty! I was robbed! All the desks, chairs, and computers were gone. I ran to my private office to find everything was missing. Even my nicknacks and personal pictures were taken.

I picked up the phone and called the police.

"Ms. Amor, do you know anyone who may want to rob you?"

I told the officer about my text conversation with my bookkeeper and the condition I found my house in.

"Could you tell us a little bit about her?"

"Yes, I could give you her personnel files." *At least they didn't take the cabinets.* I walked to the file cabinet that kept the employee records opened the drawer. Empty! "They took their files." I began to open all the drawers in the cabinets. All of them were empty. "They took all the files. Everything. Personnel files. Clients. Contracts. Everything!" As my mind tried to wrap around what was going on, the phone rang. "Hello?"

"Ms. Amor? This is Mr. Lopez from the bank. There seems to be an issue with your account, ma'am."

"What issue?"

"Your account is overdrawn over $5000

dollars. We have put a stop on all payments until the situation is resolved. Could you please come down to the bank so we could straighten this out?"

Wait, I have close to seven figures in that account. How could ... The checks! I had left the checks with Jane to handle any unforeseen expenses. I explained the phone call from the bank to the officers.

It turns out that Jane was in cahoots with two of my senior sales staff. They had waited until I was away and then fired the whole staff, sold all my equipment, and embezzled the company money from my bank account. I was forced to close the office and start again. All my years of hard work was gone.

I was devastated.

"Fall down seven times, get up eight."
- Old Japanese Proverb

I had two choices after that. I could either give up or I could get up!

I decided to get back up. The first thing I

needed to do was find some way to make peace with the betrayal. I began to pray and meditate. I took long walks on the beach to calm my mind and spirit. I knew I couldn't move forward if I held on to my anger at Jane and the situation. Anger is drinking a cup of poison and expecting the other person to die.

I took a good, hard look in the "soul mirror" and gave myself an Honesty Check. *What lessons could I learn from this situation? How could I become a stronger person?*

I had a bunch of books, CDs, and DVDs lying around from the various seminars and workshops I attended over the years. The Secret. What the Bleep Do We Know. Awaken the Giant Within. I watched and rewatched, read and reread them and took note of everything that would help me manifest the life I wanted.

I started a daily Gratitude Journal to help me focus on what I was thankful for in life and reinforce good thought patterns.

I changed my mindset.

When I think of all that I had to go through, I realize that everything really works out in the end. It's been over five years since those events and I am glad I utilized The Power to Get Back Up. I now run a business where I inspire and empower others. I am happily married to the best man in the world, and I have friends and business partners who I truly trust and love.

2. The Power of Attitude

"It's your attitude not your aptitude that will determine your altitude."

- Zig Ziglar

Losing everything I had put me in a deep depression. I had still not recovered any property or money and my former employees could not be found. My lawyer advised me to move on, telling me that they may never be located. At the same time my visa was getting ready to expire and there was a good chance I was going to be deported from the country. I had no money to my name. My Negative Ball was throwing a party. I believe that everything happens for a reason and that if God brings you to it, he'll bring you through it. I knew there was a reason I was going through these issues and even though I couldn't see it, I focused on these thoughts and kept my attitude positive. It was not easy.

My mother knew I was depressed and paid for me to visit her in Israel for a month. When the month was over, my mother gave me some money and I returned to New York where I was seeing some clients.

I was scheduled to meet a client in Brooklyn early one morning and decided to leave a little early and check out the avenue for a place to grab breakfast. After spending so long in Israel I was craving bacon and eggs. I stopped at a place called The Donut Stop. It looked clean and had an "A" rating sign in the window. I walked in and saw the guy behind the counter. He was about six feet tall, bald, and dressed in a tee shirt and khakis. *He's cute.* He walked up to me and I felt my heart skip a beat.

"Do you want some coffee?" He lifted the pot

of coffee he was holding.

"No. Cappuccino, please" I pointed to the machine sitting on the counter. "And some bacon and eggs."

He smiled. "Coming right up."

A few minutes later my cappuccino and food arrived.

"Are you from around here? I don't recognize you."

"No. I come here on business a few days every month."

I stayed an hour longer than I should have and we talked while I ate. His name was Alex and he was the owner of the coffee shop. He cooked for and served his other customers while we talked and always came back to check on me.

After I finished eating, I paid and left. Something told me I would be back to this coffee shop.

The next morning I cancelled my pilates
session and found myself at The Donut Stop again.
The store was your typical neighborhood coffee shop.
It had a counter top with stools and a few tables
along the far wall. A wire news rack sat in front of a
display of donuts held the daily editions of the New
York Post, Daily News, and New York Times.

I sat drinking my coffee, watching television.
My eyes followed Alex as he handled the customers
that came into his shop. Just looking at him made me
feel squishy inside. I didn't need to talk with him, just
watching him cook at the grill top was enough.

After a few hours I needed to leave for some
meetings. I paid for my coffee and, before I left, I
handed Alex my business card.

"I'll call you," he said. "Maybe we could grab
some coffee."

"I leave tomorrow morning for Florida. Maybe
when I come back," I said and left the store.

After my meetings were finished I took the

subway back to Brooklyn and returned home. I opened the front door and put my stuff down. My roommate Susan walked into the room.

"So, do you have any plans for the night?"

"I think I might have a date," I said.

"Orly, you don't know anybody here. How could you have a date?"

I told her about the last two days and meeting Alex. She just shook her head in disbelief. I walked back to my bedroom to unwind and wait for the call.

I was home for a few hours when my cell phone rang. It was Alex.

"Hey, I thought we could go for some coffee later."

"I'd like that."

"The shop closes at nine, so I'll pick you up then."

"I'll be out front waiting for you."

I burst into the living room screaming like a

school girl. "He called! I've got a date!"

Susan shook her head. "How do you do that?"

"Do what?" I replied.

"After everything you've been through, you still remain upbeat and positive. And everything just works out for you. You've been in Brooklyn for less than a month, you don't know anyone and yet you have a date tonight. I haven't had a date in months. How do you do that?"

"I just believe and have faith that everything will work out. If God leads you to it, he'll lead you through it."

Alex and I had coffee and talked all night. When I told him I needed to go home to pack and wait for the car service to take me to the airport, he had me cancel the service and drove me home. He waited for me to pack and then drove me to the airport himself. Before I boarded my plane we promised to see each other again when I returned to Brooklyn.

We met for coffee again when I came back and have had coffee together almost every day since.

On March 10, 2013 we were married.

Situations, events, and circumstances are neither good nor bad, but how we think about them makes them so. It is attitude, not circumstance, that makes success possible in even the most unlikely conditions. Your past does not equal your future for the simple reason that in each moment you have the power to choose who to feed. Do you want to feed the Negative Ball, or do you want to nourish your Positive Ball?

In order to nourish your Positive Ball you need to change your attitude. You need to unpack your victim's bag and change your thinking from "Why do these things always happen to me?" to "What is great about this?" and "What can I learn from this?"

Have understanding and compassion for yourself.

After the events I shared with you in the

previous chapter, I needed to release the anger I was holding towards my employees and myself. I had to realize that there was no tracking them down and just let it go. It was my poor attitude that was feeding the Negative Ball and preventing me from moving forward. I needed to focus on nourishing the Positive Ball.

I realized I had attracted this incident into my life because of my insecurities. I accused myself of being stupid, naive and much more. I had to stop those personal attacks because they fed the Negative Ball. I cannot control other people. I can only control myself. So I needed to become my own best friend.

I started asking questions that would change my attitude. Instead of asking "why" questions, I asked "what" questions.

- "Why did Jane and the others do this to me?" became "What do I love and respect about Jane and the others?"

- "Why am I always so trusting?" became "What do I gain from being a positive person?"

• "Why do I need to start again after years of hard work?" became "What could I create that could help others?"

• "Why do these things happen to me?" became "What lessons could I learn from this?"

In addition to asking new and different questions, I needed to look at the truth without any drama. When we focus on the drama we blow things up larger than they are and the Negative Ball feasts on a supersized meal. I searched for the gifts in each circumstance. I searched outside my immediate situation to the bigger picture. I looked into my heart to find compassion and became my own best friend.

3. The Power of Self-Talk

"No problem can be solved from the same level of consciousness that created it."
— *Albert Einstein*

When I was in high school I had a boyfriend. After graduation, he broke up with me. When I asked him why he told me, "You have a beautiful personality but your body leaves a lot to be desired."

I already had body image issues and his blunt statement didn't help me. The Negative Ball started shouting.

"You're too fat."

"You're too ugly."

"No one will want you."

"No one will love you."

My self-esteem dropped. I became depressed. I thought about ending my life.

I needed to nourish my Positive Ball.

It was then I discovered the Power of Self-Talk.

Self-talk is the food of the Positive and Negative Balls. It has the power of starving one while nourishing the other.

Shakespeare wrote that, "there is nothing good or bad, but thinking makes it so." (Hamlet: Act 2, Scene 2) How we think about ourselves determines which Ball we feed. When we fill our thoughts and self-talk with doubts and fear, the Negative Ball grows fat.

We must learn to nourish our Positive Ball through affirmative self-talk and gratitude.

In one of my mindset workshops a woman stood up and said, "I have been praying to win the lottery forever. I have bought tickets every week. I pray every day. I go to church every week. I give to charity and I do everything I am told to do, but I have yet to see the million dollars I have been praying for."

I asked her if I gave her one million dollars right now would she be able to take it from me without saying thank you.

She looked at me as if I had two heads and after a moment she answered, "No."

"That is why you don't have that one million dollars."

Her self-talk and thoughts were that she was not worthy of the million dollars. She was focusing on her needs and fears and feeding her Negative Ball.

Fear is an emotion that is created from the unknown. When you focus your thoughts and self talk on having faith that everything will work out, why you do deserve these things, and be gentle with yourself when unexpected results arise you will nourish your Positive Ball.

Isn't it true that we sometimes worry so much for nothing? Did you ever hear yourself say, "Oh boy, I can't believe I worried so much?"

Faith and fear cannot hold the same space. When you nourish your Positive Ball through positive self-talk you eliminate fear and starve the Negative Ball.

Here are some steps you may follow to increase your positive self-talk:

- Treat yourself with respect and kindness.

- Tell yourself that you are worthy of all the abundance the Universe offers and have faith you will receive it.

- Surround yourself with people who love and encourage you.

Surrounding yourself with loving people who will support and encourage you nourishes your Positive Ball. It is an important way to reinforce your positive thoughts and self-talk. We all need that support system to pick us up and remind us we are worthy of success and abundance.

A friend of mine who wanted to lose weight, asked me to support her on her journey. The program she decided to follow let her be present, eat right, exercise all week and on Sunday, allowed her to indulge. I thought it was a great idea. After the first few weeks she had lost twenty pounds and was proud of herself. This success created positive self-talk and nourished her Positive Ball. One Sunday, she went to a family get together. After dinner they served chocolate cake for dessert.

"How nice," she thought. As she helped herself to a piece of cake, one family member said, "Are you really going to eat that? You've been doing so well on your diet. You don't want to ruin everything you worked so hard for."

My friend burst out crying. In one "well meaning" statement this family member destroyed all her positive thoughts and self-talk and her Negative Ball rejoiced. My friend had been working diligently to lose the weight and was feeling good about her progress. Her Negative Ball was being starved by her success. If the family member was truly being supportive they might have suggested that they go for a walk after dinner.

Do not let others feed the Negative Ball. Believe in yourself and nourish your Positive Ball with positive self-talk. If someone is not caring and supportive of you do not let them know your plans, hopes, or aspirations. Surround yourself only with people who will support and encourage you. They will help nourish your Positive Ball.

4. The Power of Honesty

"Honesty is the first chapter in the book of wisdom."
- Thomas Jefferson

I laid on the bed in the guest room of my house in Montreal after it was over crying. A family member just had his way with me. Forcibly.

I was 20 years old and this was the third time a man had raped me. My dress was torn and marks and bruises covered me.

Feelings of guilt, shame, and anger washed over me. *How could I let this happen again?* I wanted to die. I pushed the pain down so far, I forgot it existed. I went on with my life as if nothing had happened. No one knew what I was going through, but everything around me became doom and gloom.

The Negative Ball flourished in my denial. I reached morbid obesity and a weight of 428 pounds. I constantly gave myself excuses about why it was okay to be morbidly obese. I told myself that I have been through so much, that people were judging me without knowing my story.

I blamed my family, my coworkers, and everybody I could think of for my downfall, but the truth was I wasn't looking at my feelings and being honest about them. One day I realized that I was in control of all those thoughts and feelings and how this horrifying story ends was entirely up to me and me alone.

I had to stop feeding the Negative Ball and start nourishing my Positive Ball. I needed to stand in front of the "soul mirror" and admit my feelings and fears. Once I did this, I could start working on healing. And loving myself again.

This is a crucial step that absolutely needs to be taken. If you do not know where you are, how can you possibly know where you are going? How will you recognize what you need to do in order to reach your destination and how will you know when you have arrived?

Who or what are you blaming for the way things are in your life?

No matter where you find yourself at this very moment you must be truthful about it and write it all down. Right now, take out a sheet of paper and take an inventory of your life. Are you where you want to be financially? Spiritually? Materialistically? Where would you like to be in each area of your life? Be ready to take inventory of what works and what doesn't work for you. Address the things that do not work honestly and ask yourself how you can improve upon them. Take responsibility for the part you played in creating your present situation. Forgive yourself and then move forward. Find the solution and apply what you have learned.

Now is the time to be honest and plan your

life. With a plan in place you have a direction.

And with a plan in place you will nourish your Positive Ball.

5. The Power of Taking Action

"A dream becomes a goal when action is taken towards its achievement."

- Bo Bennett

There is a story about a man who every morning while taking a walk, passed by this house where an older gentleman and his wife were sitting on a porch. The gentleman read the newspaper and his wife just rocked away. Between them was a dog lying on the floor crying and whining. It was pitiful and heartbreaking to see and hear. The man continued on walking, troubled by what he'd seen. Every day as the man walked by, the scene was the same, the older gentleman and his wife sat on the porch; the gentleman read the newspaper and his wife rocked away. The dog was lying between them on the floor crying and whining.

This went on for about a week. The man, feeling sorry for the dog in pain, decided that if tomorrow he walked by and the scene was still the same, he would ask about the dog.

The next morning as he was taking his walk, the scene was the same. The older gentleman and his wife were sitting on the porch. The gentleman read the newspaper and his wife rocked away. Between them was the dog lying on the floor crying and whining. The man approached the wife and said, "Excuse me, ma'am. What is wrong with your dog?" She answered, "Oh him? He is lying on a nail."

Perplexed by her response the man asked, "Well, why doesn't he move?"

The woman responded, "Well you see dear, it is hurting him enough to cry and whine about it, but not hurting him enough to move."

My nail story was my weight.

As I told you in the previous chapter, I reached a weight of 428 pounds after I was raped. This severely impacted my social and dating life. I complained that no man would ever find me attractive or love me, but I had not reached the point where I was willing to take action and change it. I was happy complaining about my situation and feeding the Negative Ball.

Tony Robbins says that change only takes place once we reach our threshold of pain. If something was going to change about my weight, I needed to move through my pain threshold. It takes a little bit of anger and frustration with a situation or behavior for us to actually take action. I needed to gain leverage over my pain and use it to change and nourish my Positive Ball.

I used the rejection from men and the snide remarks and dirty looks I received at Publix to gain leverage and take action to lose the weight.

What nail are you lying on?

What is it costing you?

How satisfied are you with that area of your life?

When I work with my clients, one of the first exercises I do with them is the Pain Threshold test.

I want you to get a sheet a paper and write down how much you are willing to learn to change the part of your life that you are not happy with. Use a scale of 1 to 10, where one is not at all willing to learn and ten is absolutely willing to learn. Next, I want you to write down how much you are willing to change. How much are you willing to sacrifice in order to achieve the change you want. Again, use a scale of 1 to 10, where one is not at all willing to change/sacrifice and ten is absolutely willing to change/sacrifice. Now multiply those two numbers. The higher the number, the closer you are to threshold and change.

For example, with my weight, I was at a 10 to

learn and an 8 to change/sacrifice. So, my pain threshold level was at an 80. I absolutely had to change.

What is your number? If it is under 50, you are like the dog sitting on the nail. Your life is not where you want it, but it's not so bad that you must change it.

So, how do you get from less than 50 to over 50 and close to 100 so change stops being a should and becomes a must? How do you get yourself to take action? You increase your pain threshold towards the situation that needs changing. When your pain threshold gets closer to 100, your brain automatically searches for ways to release it. At this point, we show your brain the door out of pain.

Think about an area of your life that you want to change but haven't taken any action on. Maybe it's your finances, or your weight, or your relationships. Now go through the Pain Threshold exercise.

On a scale of 1-10, how willing are you to

learn how to change this area of your life? Write it down.

On a scale of 1-10, how willing are you to actually do what is necessary to change? How willing are you to sacrifice and give up something or do something that's required to create the change you want? Write it down.

Most people will score high on their willingness to learn how to change, but low on their willingness to sacrifice and actually create that change.

Now let's increase that willingness to sacrifice and create the necessary change number.

Close your eyes and imagine what this situation or behavior that must change is costing you. What if the situation that needs changing is your finances? Imagine having no money in the bank and then finding out your mother is terminally ill. How does it feel to know you can't be with her during her last moments? Maybe the situation is, like mine was, your weight? Imagine all the health issues and medical costs you will have because you are overweight.

Maybe you are stuck in an abusive relationship. Imagine all the pain you are receiving from staying with this person. How does this feel?

Now, write all these statements down on a piece of paper. Write down all the painful things you will experience if you do not change your thoughts and feelings towards the situation.

Can you feel your pain levels rise? Good. Now let's show your brain the door out.

Close your eyes again. This time imagine that the situation or behavior that must change has indeed changed. You have an abundance of money so you can spend as much time with your mom as you want. You are at the ideal weight and you feel fantastic. You are in a healthy relationship with a loving, supportive person. How does this feel?

Next, write all these statements down on a piece of paper. Write down all the wonderful things you are experiencing because you took action and changed the situation.

Now take the Pain Threshold test again. Did

your "willingness to change" number increase? I bet it did.

6. The Power of Knowledge

"To know and not to do is not to know at all."
- Leo Buscaglia

People often say that knowledge is power, but
the truth is that knowledge alone cannot bring about
change. You must take action on what you know. I
first was introduced to The Law of Attraction from
the movie The Secret. One of the basic tenets of The
Law of Attraction is that "like attracts like." I
watched the DVD hundreds of time and listened to
the CD in my car constantly. Even with all this, I was
still skeptical so I decided to actually test it. I started
with small things like, finding my keys, getting
someone to take me out for coffee or lunch, etc. I

found that when I applied the principles, everything just worked.

I soon moved on to larger experiments.

In my office I used to say, "What Orly Wants, Orly Gets." I told my employees about the Law of Attraction and I had them finish the sentence whenever I would ask for something ridiculous. I would say "What Orly Wants …"

They would complete the sentence with "… Orly Gets." By the way, it was not said with enthusiasm. They all thought I was crazy to even think that way.

One time we were putting together a seminar for about 260 people in the property management industry. The goal was to sell enough sponsorships and exhibitor tables to cover the costs and, of course, make money.

On a Tuesday afternoon after a long day of meetings, I got to the office around 4 PM and asked my team where we were for that week as far as sales. They gave me a report that showed less than $3000.

I told them we needed $10,000 by Friday that week. They looked at me as if I had three heads and said, "No way. It's not possible. That means we have less then three days."

My response? "What Orly Wants …"

They responded with a most angry tone, "Yeah, yeah … Orly gets."

I left them and went to my office to continue working.

A couple of days later, I asked if we had made any progress. With a frown on their faces they answered, "not really."

The secretary was out sick that day, so my next question was, "Did anyone get the mail today?"

I received a look that shot daggers across the room. Finally, one of them said, "You want us to close with $10,000 by tomorrow and you seriously think we have time for the mail?"

I did not respond. I simply grabbed the keys and went to the mailbox. When I returned I took the mail into my office and started to open the envelopes. The first one was a letter. The second, an invoice.

The third piece of mail had a check of $8,734 from an unpaid invoice that was six months overdue. I took the check, faced it towards my team and walked around the office showing it off. Their reaction was priceless.

"How do you do this? How do you always make it happen for yourself?"

The answer: I do not simply read books. I apply what I read; therefore my knowledge is used to change my circumstances.

"There is nothing like returning to a place that is unchanged to find the ways in which you, yourself are altered."
- Nelson Mandela

Sometimes the knowledge we receive is information, sometimes it is confirmation.

It is not only important to apply what you know, but to realize that we always change and grow, so what we learned years ago we look at with new eyes each time we are exposed to it.

In 2004, I was speaking at a Real Estate seminar in San Diego given by the stars of some very popular television shows. I was opening and closing the weekend. On Friday, I was speaking on the importance of mindset in sales. I asked how many people had read The Power of Positive Thinking by Norman Vincent Peale. Almost every hand in the room shot up. At the same time, a voice from the back shouted, "Yeah, yeah, yeah. I read it years ago. I got nothing from it."

I asked the gentlemen to come to the front of the room and asked him his name. He told me it was Mike.

"Mike," I began. "You know, they have updated and revised the book in recent years. Would you be willing to buy a copy this weekend and just read a few stories and tell us if you learned something from the newer version?"

Mike agreed.

On Sunday I was back on stage to close the conference. I asked if everyone was having a good time and asked if Mike was in the room. I saw him jump up and down and holler from the back of the room. I again asked him to come to the stage. "So Mike, did you buy a copy of the updated version of the book?"

"Yes I did, Orly."

"And what did you think of the new version?"

"Oh my God! They changed and added so much! I got so much value just from reading a few chapters. Thank you for suggesting it."

I smiled. "Mike, let me tell you something. That book has never been updated or revised since it was published in 1952. It's the same as it was when you read it all those years ago. What changed was you. You are no longer the same person you were back then so you received the information differently."

We are all the product of our experiences and

those experiences create our beliefs and define who we are. You gain new knowledge at each stage of life and this changes who you are. People thought the world was flat before Columbus sailed. They thought that the Sun revolved around the Earth and that Earth was the center of the universe before Copernicus. After these discoveries no one could look at the world the same way again. This new knowledge forever changed the way humans viewed themselves and led to new thoughts.

Columbus' discovery led to a business and financial boom in trade and the discovery of new people.

Copernicus' discovery led man to look at the skies differently and eventually led to space flight, Alan Shepard, and Neil Armstrong.

Always take the time to review what you previously learned. Re-read the books and listen to the CDs and tapes again and again. Remember you are a different person now than you were when you first were exposed to them and because of this you will gain new insights.

How will looking at the knowledge you gained in the past with new eyes change your life?

7. The Power of Why

"The journey of a thousand miles starts with a single
step"
- Lao Tzu

In 2001, I was still 428 pounds. I still had self
image issues and was worried over having a heart
attack or getting diabetes. I had reached my Pain
Threshold and started to look at surgery as an option
to fix the issue. There were two surgeries available.
Lap band surgery and gastric bypass. My doctor told
me that three out of five people who have gastric
bypass surgery died on the table. It was the more
dangerous one. I chose to have the lap band surgery.

I was living in Montreal and lap band surgery

was still a new procedure at the time. There were no bands available in Canada so they would need to be ordered from California. The band cost over $4500. In addition, there were no hospital beds available for two years. This means I would need to wait for two years to correct my weight issue. I knew I needed to get control of this so I may lead a long, healthy life. This was my "why," and it drove me to pursue the surgery.

My doctor told me that I would not have to pay until there was a hospital bed available and the lap band arrived. I started to save the money for the surgery. And then 9/11 happened. After the attacks on the World Trade Center everything was pushed back or delayed indefinitely. I still was certain about having the surgery but now I was in a holding pattern.

In 2002, I moved to Florida to get away from the cold. While the warmth of the Miami sun was a blessing, this reset my plans for the lap band surgery but I never let go of my why. My why remained part of who I was. It drove me.

In 2003, I was visiting a girlfriend in New York City. Anna was a dear friend of mine who I hadn't seen in years. We were leaving Serendipity when she turned to me and said, "Orly, you know you walk like a duck."

I know she didn't mean anything by it but it fed the Negative Ball. *I feel like the Goodyear Blimp.* I decided then to start looking into surgery again.

In 2004, my assistant knew I was considering surgery to correct my weight issues and mentioned that she knew a doctor that performed gastric bypass surgery in Colombia. Even though it was the more evasive option, I had waited long enough. I asked her to come with me to meet with the doctor and his team because I was not fluent in Spanish.

The doctor's office was beautiful. The anesthesiologist told me I had a perfectly healthy stomach.

On June 2, 2005, I had my surgery.

When we pursue our dreams and goals there will be challenges we will face. How we respond and react to those challenges depends on how strong our "why" is. The reason people do not achieve their goals is they do not have a strong enough why. Most people's "why" is an intellectual reason. Their reasons do not live with them. They do not feel them in their soul.

Many people want to lose weight but after two weeks they give up. They say they want to be healthy but those reasons are not rooted in their "why." Their "why" needs to be born from moving through threshold and gaining leverage.

This is the same reason New Year's Resolutions often fail. There are things people believe they need to do but they have no reason why they must do it, so by February 15th, the gyms are empty.

What is your "Why?"

Your "why" must be strong enough to motivate you to follow through and do whatever it takes to achieve success. It must be strong enough to starve the Negative Ball and nourish your Positive Ball.

When your "why's" are strong enough, the "how's" will follow.

8. The Power of Consistency

"Success isn't always about greatness. It's about consistency. Consistent hard work leads to success. Greatness will come."
- Dwayne "The Rock" Johnson

The first two weeks after my surgery I was on a liquid diet. Over the next six months, I progressed from a liquid diet to a mushy diet to being able to eat solid foods. This was part of the recovery from the surgery. During this time I had lost 85 pounds. For the first time I could remember, I was under 350 pounds. I attended my cousin's wedding in Montreal and everyone complimented me on the way I looked. My Positive Ball was singing!

When I was able to eat solid foods again, I began to gain weight. I would not let that happen.

I changed my behavior.

I stopped eating bread. I stopped drinking soda. I stopped eating after seven o'clock in the evening. I hired a personal trainer and started to work out everyday. I also worked on nourishing my Positive Ball. I performed daily affirmations and wrote down 100 things I was grateful for everyday. I watched TED Talks, and listened to The Secret.

All this took determination and consistency. I had to recommit myself to my goal everyday. Rain or shine, I was at the gym. Everyday I wrote my affirmations, meditated and prayed, and worked out. There were times I was sick and could barely get out of bed, but I pushed myself to go to the gym.

My "why" drove me, but it was my consistency of action that got the results. Two years later, I weighed 210 pounds.

I had a client who went through my Mindset

Mastery program. The program was designed for executives who wanted to learn how to become more efficient, communicate more effectively, inspire their teams, and take their business to the next level. A few weeks after she finished, she called me.

"Hey Orly!"

"Hi, Julie. How may I help you?"

"You told me I needed to set ambitious goals. I wanted to let you know that I decided to run the New York City Marathon."

"That's great," I said. Julie had never run for anything but a crosstown bus before, but now she was going to run a marathon? I wanted to know why. How did this transformation happen? She told me that she wanted to get into shape and running sounded like a good way to do so. She told me she joined a local gym that trained runners and that she was going to take it slow.

For the next few years Julie trained everyday and was soon running 5Ks. 5K races became 10K races. Julie graduated to half marathons. She ran five of them. Everyday she would get up and run before starting her day and would go to the gym to train before heading home; all to reach her goal of running in the New York City Marathon.

On November 3, 2013 she crossed the finish line in front of Tavern on the Green in six hours, twenty-two minutes, and twenty-five seconds.

Consistency will nourish your Positive Ball.

Consistency creates momentum. By focusing on one thing and never faltering in your vision you will be able to measure your progress. You can see how far you have come towards achieving your goal. Consistency also helps nourish your Positive Ball by reinforcing the positive self-talk you will get from working towards your goals and seeing your progress. It creates your reputation. When you act consistently and always do what you say you will do, people will see you as dependable and reliable and your Positive Ball will smile.

It takes twenty-one days to change a habit.

Twenty-one days of nourishing your Positive Ball.

Twenty-one days of taking action to move you towards your goal.

When you take consistent action you tap into a power greater than the action itself. You nourish your Positive Ball with the belief that you are completely capable of changing the behavior.

What do you want to achieve?

Is there a time you can remember when you decided that no matter what you were going to make a change? How did you achieve this? You used your Powers. The Power of Attitude. The Power of Knowledge. The Power of Why. Using these Powers you gained leverage on your goal but you still needed to take consistent action to make it happen.

You can get anything you want by just taking consistent action. Set a goal and create a plan to achieve it. Then take action every day towards it.

9. The Power of Forgiveness

"The weak can never forgive. Forgiveness is the attribute of the strong."
- Mahatma Gandhi

We learn something from every experience, event and circumstance in our lives. What works and what doesn't, what we like and what we don't like, there may even be a lesson that will serve us in the future.

In 2005, Hurricane Wilma hit the Florida Coast. Most of the properties I was managing were damaged. I was on site at one property in Ft. Lauderdale that had severe structural damage to the building. Cracks, windows blown out, doors broken.

A ficus tree had been uprooted and pulled the main transformer out of the ground. 240 residents were without power.

I was working 20 hours a day, seven days a week assessing the damage, creating solutions, and assuring the residents that we were doing everything possible to return to normalcy. These residents were displaced and were not happy. Since I was on site for the owner, I became the focus of their anger and frustration.

During this time, the owner of the property was calling me wanting to know which residents paid their rent, which hadn't, and how much he was still owed. I explained that the whole property was damaged by the hurricane and was without power so I had no way of getting him the information. Still, every five or ten minutes my phone would ring and it would be him demanding the information. I began to feel angry and overwhelmed. I felt alone in the world. Between the residents and the property's owner, I had no peace.

For close to a month, I would go to bed at night, wake up in the morning, go to work every day, and I could not even recognize enjoyment for what it was. I was exhausted. It got so bad that I threw my flip phone across the room. It hit the wall and shattered. *At least I won't get any more calls from the owner!*

After a week or two, I realized that the Negative Ball had taken over my life. I was angry, resentful, and frustrated all the time. I didn't like who I was becoming. I went home and decided to change. I decided to nourish my Positive Ball.

How? I decided to forgive all the people. I decided to forgive the residents for taking their frustrations out on me. They had just had their lives turned upside down. I decided to forgive the owner because he was not on site and had no idea of the level of devastation that Hurricane Wilma brought.

Immediately, I felt a weight lift off of me. I realized that people do not know what they do not know. The residents did not know how diligently I was working to fix their homes. The owner did not know the amount of damage the property had because he was not on site.

I was able to work more efficiently and effectively and be more present for the residents once I focused on what I could control. So I forgave.

Take your emotional pulse right now.

How do you feel? Are you carrying any anger or resentment? How about jealousy and sadness? If so, find it in your heart to forgive. There is no need to forget because there is a lesson to be learned. You only have to forgive.

"But Orly, I really am having a challenge with forgiving, especially if I did not deserve the wrong that was done to me."

Well dear friend, you must still forgive. Tell yourself that this person did not know better. That he/she/they are ignorant. Just move on, because if you don't, the Negative Ball will enjoy the ride and will make sure to create more events and circumstances to make you feel this way again and again and again.

Remember, misery does love company.

It is up to you to be aware of the feelings you carry around. At the end of the day, you are the one that goes to sleep with those feelings. Learn to recognize your positive feelings and your negative ones. What past issues may be causing negative self-talk and feeding the Negative Ball by creating negative feelings? Forgive the people those issues revolve around. Especially if one of those people is you. Practice self-love and start forgiving yourself.

The past is dead and gone and does not have any impact on the future unless you let it.

When you learn to forgive, you chase away all your negative thoughts. You starve the Negative Ball. When you forgive, you will feel much better and your Positive Ball will grow healthy and strong.

10. The Power of Choice

"It is our choices, Harry, that define what we truly are,
far more than our abilities"
- JK Rowling (Harry Potter and the Chamber of
Secrets)

There's a story in the book, The Power of
Positive Thinking.

A 90 year old man was known never to
experience a bad day in his life. He was always happy,
upbeat, and positive. His friends and family could not
understand how this man never experienced a bad
day in his life. They thought he found the Magic
Formula to Happiness. One day, the man was invited
to appear on a television show. The host asked him if

he knew why he was invited to the show.

"No," the man replied. "But I'm happy to be here."

The host explained that his friends and family wrote about his amazing ability to always be happy and he was there to share his secrets and wisdom with the audience and viewers.

The man thought for a moment and then started to speak. "Well, every morning I look at my two hands and decide whether I want to be happy or not to be happy. And then I choose to be happy."

The host was flabbergasted. "That's it?"

The old man nodded. "That's it."

Psychoanalyst Victor Frankl was a Holocaust survivor. He survived Auschwitz and Dachau while his brother, mother and wife perished. In his book, "Man's Search for Meaning", he wrote, "Everything can be taken from a man but one thing, the last of the human freedoms - to choose one's attitude in any given set of circumstances, to choose one's own way."

Frankl chose to live so that others may know of the horrors of the camp. This became his "why." He chose to use the Power of Why to survive the many atrocities of Auschwitz and Dachau to make sure it never happened again.

In every moment we have the Power of Choice.

We can choose to be happy or we can choose to miserable. We could choose to be grateful or we could choose to be envious.

When I was raped by my ex-husband, he almost killed me. At that moment I had a choice to make. Either I could die or I could live.

I chose to live. I decided the reason I was going through all the hurt, agony, and emotional turmoil was for a reason. I needed to live so that I could tell my story and change people's lives.

This was my choice. It was my choice to hold my head up high. I chose to not let the rape define me.

It's all in the mind and in the choice.

No matter how bad your situation is, remember, you are always in control. You can choose your thoughts. You can choose your actions.

What are your needs? What are your wants and desires? Write them down. Put them all on paper. Now look at that paper. Realize you are in control and you can achieve your goals. You have the choice to make them all come true or to complain about why you do not have them.

When you choose to complain you will be full of should haves, could haves, and would haves.

You give away your Power.

You feed the Negative Ball.

You must learn to choose positive action. When you choose action and positive self-talk, you nourish your Positive Ball. Choose to use The Power of Honesty and look at your life. Discover your negative emotions and choose to let them go. Think of yourself as an onion with many layers. Each layer is an emotion attached to an experience, event, or circumstance and you are peeling it away one layer at a time.

With the Power of Choice you can address each layer and get rid of it until you find the essence of blissful feelings and the calm that comes after the storm.

11. The Power of Focus

"Stay focused, go after your dreams and keep moving toward your goals."
- LL Cool J

Multi-tasking is a myth.

The brain was not designed to perform many tasks at the same time. The more tasks we take on, the more balls we attempt to juggle, the less effective our brains become. Did you ever pick up a ringing phone while typing a report?

What happened? If you're like most people, you lost focus and couldn't remember what you were typing.

We tend to take on several projects and lose

focus. We become overwhelmed. Overwhelm leads to procrastination and resentment. Suddenly those goals we were so excited about become our albatross. We lose interest in doing them and we start to beat ourselves up over not achieving anything we start.

The Negative Ball gets fed.

This book that you're reading is an example of The Power of Focus.

When I started writing it, I was excited. It was my passion project. I wanted to share my insights with everyone and empower their lives. Then my life got busy. I started to get more and more public speaking opportunities. From those gigs I got several new clients for my coaching business. I created The Health and Wellness Network of Commerce, an organization dedicated to bridging the gap between Corporate America and Health and Wellness practitioners. This required running several expos and networking events every month. The organization quickly grew; being in nine states and six countries around the world. When each new Chapter opened, I needed to be there to welcome them to the family.

I became overwhelmed as I tried to juggle all these projects. I couldn't focus on writing and give it the necessary attention. The book suffered.

Then I received a call from my publisher. "Orly, how's the book coming along?"

"It's coming. I'm really busy with some other things so I haven't been able to write as much as I want."

"Orly, we are coming up on the deadline. If we don't have the book by the end of the month we won't be able to meet the goal of releasing it on December 12th. We'll have to push the release back by at least six months."

My mind went blank. I needed the book to be released on December 12th. 12/12. 12 Powers. Get it? I didn't want to wait six months. I needed to finish the book and get it to my publisher. I needed to hit the deadline. I needed to focus.

I placed some of my newer projects on the back burner, and delegated some of my responsibilities to my assistants. I shifted my daily schedule around to free up solid chunks of time where I could write uninterrupted, and focused on completing the book.

I finished it with time to spare and you are holding the results in your hands.

Focus means Follow One Course Until Success.

If we want to be successful and achieve, we need to let go of our desire to multitask. Society has sold us on busyness. Busyness is not effective, nor is it efficient. We all run around from one thing to the next and believe we are being productive but nothing gets accomplished. This is how the feeling of overwhelm happens and how the Negative Ball gets fed.

When we focus on completing one task instead of multitasking, we see the constant march towards the finish line of our goal. As we get closer, we start to feel more accomplished and proud. Our stress levels decrease. We also feel more in control and can make better decisions when we focus on one task. We eliminate distraction.

Focus can also increase our happiness. A 2010 study published in Science magazine showed that Harvard researchers tracked the happiness levels of over 2,200 people from around the world through an iPhone app. The participants were asked to rate their levels of happiness at random times, report what activity they were doing, and tell whether they were focused on the task or daydreaming.

They received over 250,000 responses. The results were eye-opening.

Almost 47% of the time respondents were not focused on what they were doing. And those people whose mind wandered reported a lower level of happiness than those who were focused on a specific task. It didn't matter if people were daydreaming about pleasant activities or focused on mundane tasks, such as grocery shopping. Those people who were focused on a task consistently rated their happiness levels higher.

Their happiness was not connected to what they were doing but how attentive and mindful they were while doing it.

If you want to be happy, stay focused on one task until it's complete. It'll nourish your Positive Ball.

12. The Power of Happiness

"Happiness is not something you postpone for the future; it is something you design for the present."

- Jim Rohn

Ask anyone who knows me and they will tell you I love to laugh. Not chuckles, but huge, loud belly laughs. As a kid, I would laugh so hard at jokes that no one else found funny. I'd laugh so hard that I shot orange juice out of my nose. To me, laughter is an expression of my joy and happiness with life. During all the challenges in my life, I held the thought that everyday above ground is a good day in the front of my mind. That thought allowed me to remain happy and grateful no matter what else was going on. It allowed me to starve the Negative Ball and nourish my Positive Ball.

As we grow older, we lose that childlike state of awe and wonder and joy. People hurt us. They let us down. We sometimes fail at what we do. We carry all the baggage of our negative experiences and responsibilities with us. They weigh us down. We no longer find joy in the little things because we are busy worrying about the bigger things.

Jobs. Money. Relationships.

The Negative Ball loves all this baggage. The more bags we have - the more powerful the Negative Ball becomes.

A child has little or no baggage. Their Negative Ball is small. They are always happy, always smiling, and they always laugh. No matter what.

Have you ever watched a child approach a puddle in the middle of a rainstorm? They look at it differently than adults do. A child will run up to the puddle and jump right in it, splashing water all over themselves and everything. And then laugh out loud.

You and I approach that puddle in the rainstorm and complain if we can't walk around it because our shoes will get wet.

All of our baggage has made us lose our ability to be happy. We need to become children again. We need to learn to unpack our baggage.

So how do we do that?

You might have heard of a runner's high. Many marathon runners experience this phenomenon while completing the 26.2 mile race. A runner's high is caused from the release of certain neurotransmitters such as serotonin, dopamine, and endorphins. Luckily, we do not have to run marathons to get the same effect.

Endorphins are released into our system during times of strenuous activities. Walking, running, yoga, and lifting weights all will trigger these neurochemicals.

Motion equals emotion. When the Negative Ball is flexing its muscles and you are not happy you can do some simple, quick, exercises. Doing some jumping jacks, or running in place for 45 seconds will change your state and starve the Negative Ball.

You can also increase your happiness by listening to your favorite upbeat music. Hearing our favorite song can transport us back to that happy place and triggers the same neurochemicals that strenuous exercise does. Smells can do the same thing. Have you ever smelled fresh-baked bread and immediately were back in grandma's kitchen? This is why aromatherapy is sometimes used to treat anxiety and depression. Vanilla, lavender, and sandalwood are all essential oils you can use to increase happiness in your life.

Being happy strengthens our immune system and lowers our stress levels. It allows us to be more creative and productive. It strengthens our resolve and the ability to solve problems.

When my Negative Ball grows loud and I start to get overwhelmed and frustrated, I use the practice of Shapeshifting to return to happiness and clear my mind of distractions and find the solutions. The Shapeshifting exercise is a simple one I would like to share with you.

Sit down in a comfortable position and let your arms just hang. Release the stress from your body. Focus your eyes on a point far from you. It could be a point on a wall, a rooftop, or anything. Now, empty your mind. Any thoughts, positive or negative, that enter your mind simply acknowledge and tell yourself that you will deal with it later. As each thought enters your mind, shift your gaze to another point in front of you.

Feel the air around you. Feel it filling your mouth and nostrils. Feel it against your skin, brushing against your hair. Feel your feet on the floor. Feel the solidness of the floor beneath you. Any thought that enters your mind, acknowledge and release.

Soon, with your mind and thoughts uncluttered and you in a happy state, the solution will present itself.

Before my gastric bypass surgery, I was worrying about where I would find the money to pay for it. The surgery cost $6500. I knew I needed the surgery for my health but had no idea how to raise the money. I started to panic and fall into overwhelm. *What am I going to do?*

I stopped and did 45 seconds of quick exercise to change my state and then Shapeshifted. After a few minutes, the solution came to me. I was going to ask one of my clients for an advance on the payment for my services. Even though I was scared, I knew this was the right action to take. After I explained to him why I needed the advance he was more than happy to agree to it.

And, as you know, I got my surgery.

Welcome to the Rest of Your Life

"Only I can change my life. No one can do it for me."
- Carol Burnett

Congratulations! You made it! You understand all the Power you have and how you can manifest the life you desire. The simple truth is that you know better now. You know that you have choices.

You now get it. You see how these 12 Powers can change your life.

You see that happiness is within your reach every second of every day. You can Shapeshift at anytime and solve your issues. You can create happiness within 45 seconds.

You understand that what you have allowed to

control you in the past can no longer dictate what you should do or how you should feel. You know that the Power of Attitude and Knowledge and Action are tools you can use to design your life.

You get that Gratitude can help you stay in the moment and nourish your Positive Ball; so live in gratitude, it is a direct line to your Higher Power.

You can use all these Powers right now and change your life to the one you want and deserve. Use these tools to feel joy every day. There are a thousand different paths leading to the right way to do anything. A thousand different ways to learn from each and every situation or experience. Using your powers and facing your truth is a part of the process. Remember to write things down, like your gratitude list, rather than type it out. When you write something out, you create anchors. When you write, you are actually anchoring new thoughts into your brain, where they will remain.

You have learned all this so far. Your mind has

expanded and is now ready to process more information. It is also ready to focus on what matters, so avoid dwelling on the things you cannot change, like your past. Even if you wanted to, you could not go back to what you were like before you started reading this book, because you now have new anchors.

So what are you going to focus on next?

As I mentioned earlier, it takes 21 days to create or break a habit. Focus on working on one behavior at a time.

Make it a habit to write a hundred things to be grateful for every day. Let me give you some examples:

Start with THANK YOU at the top of the page and follow each line with:

For my life

For my safety

For my health

For my freedom

For my body

For my skin

For my ability to think

For my ability to be thankful

And so on ...

Focus on staying on track. Decide what needs to be worked on and how you will reach your goal. Your Negative Ball will feel abandoned. It will begin to starve and become determined to make you fail; so stay focused at all costs.

Remember that every time you feel like giving up, every time you feel like something is wrong, when you have negative thoughts, or when harmful emotions are creeping in, that is your Negative Ball working on getting you off track. Avoid slipping backwards into old habits and patterns. This happens when we lose momentum and focus. It typically occurs when the environment that held us in that bad place is allowed to re-enter our life and influence our decision-making process and reduce our self-esteem. The Negative Ball is back in charge ... but only if you let it.

Learn to identify the 5 points of slippage:

1. Procrastination.

2. Rationalization.

3. Compromising Commitments.

4. Manipulation.

5. Reactive Behavior.

When you see the signs of slippage take action immediately to starve the Negative Ball.

1. Procrastination: Don't procrastinate. When you make a commitment to do something do it immediately or as soon as humanly possible. Get it done today somehow, some way.

2. Rationalization: Don't second-guess yourself or talk yourself out of things. Make a decision and act. If it doesn't work the way you planned, learn from it and decide to do it differently next time.

3. Compromising Commitments: Honor your integrity and commitment. Don't let other

people get you to undermine your decisions or commitments. Integrity is the major element of your success.

4.   Manipulation: Stop all the mind games and manipulation in their tracks. Do not manipulate others or allow others to manipulate you. You have a toolbox. Use it!

5.   Reactive Behavior: Learn to be proactive. Think about what your needs are and how you want to fulfill them. Use the Self-Fulfilling Prophecy approach and visualize yourself reaching your goals to make them a reality.

The bottom line is, this is the only life you will ever have or remember. It should be your life's goal to make everyone who meets you proud and honored to know you.

Watch your Self-Fulfilling Prophecies every moment of the day. They are an indication of the Negative Ball creeping up like the child sneaking behind your back to get to the cookie jar.

Don't sweat the times you let the Negative Ball in. You have been programmed to do so for many years.

Now is the time to remember this: If you fail start again, you can start your life over every single day. The best plans are revised during progress. Make sure to look at your plans and goals every day. If they are not unfolding the way you anticipated, tweak them and move forward. You did not start walking when you were born. It took some practice to get yourself up and moving. So be gentle with yourself. If you stumble, pick yourself up and keep going.

You know better now. You have the tools and the knowledge to guide you. You can never go back. You can only move forward. You may have noticed that when I used the words "I can't" or "You can't" in the book, I only used them when they were absolute truths, such as, "You can't change the past and you can't go back." Unless you can prove otherwise, these are absolute truths.

What's Next?

"Infuse your life with action. Don't wait for it to happen. Make it happen. Make your own future. Make your own hope. Make your own love. And whatever your beliefs, honor your creator, not by passively waiting for grace to come down from upon high, but by doing what you can to make grace happen ... yourself, right now, right down here on Earth."
- Bradley Whitford

How did you do? Are things starting to shift in your life? If you followed the directions in this book I'll bet they are.

So Orly, you ask, what's my next step?

Let me begin by saying this: "Whether you think you CAN or whether you think you CAN'T, you're always right."

These words alone should tell you where you are right now and why skeptical thinking keeps you in that very place. An open mind is what you need. You must make your mind receptive to these new concepts. You must have the determination to change your situation, and yes, you must put in the work. Remember that what you get out of this book is exactly what you are willing to put into practice. You need to implement your newfound knowledge in order to see positive results. That's simply how life works. You can have all the knowledge in the world but if you don't learn it and practice it, it will not serve you.

So, what will you begin to implement? Are you all in?

The inner voice – your intuition – your hunch will never, ever, steer you wrong.

That is my guarantee.

Recommended Reading List

- "The Power of Now" - By Eckhart Tolle

- "The Power of Positive Thinking" - By Norman Vincent Peale

- "Awaken The Giant Within" - By Anthony Robbins

- "The Four Agreements" - By Don Miguel Ruiz and Janet Mills

- "The Five Agreements" - By Don Miguel Ruiz and Janet Mills

- "Man's Search for Meaning" - By Victor Frankl

- "As a Man Thinketh" - By James Allen and Charles Conrad

- "The Secret" - By Rhonda Byrnes and Movie

- "What the Bleep do We Know?" The Movie

- "Think and Grow Rich" - By Napoleon Hill

- "Who Moved My Cheese?" - By Spencer Johnson and Kenneth Blanchard

- "Remember the ICE" - By Bob Nicoll

www.ingramcontent.com/pod-product-compliance
Lightning Source LLC
Chambersburg PA
CBHW061045110426
42740CB00049B/2203